Well, That Was a Doozy!

A Therapist's Guide to Participating in Life's Unexpected Moments

Rachael Stewart, LCSW

Copyright
Well, That Was a Doozy! A Therapist's Guide to Participating in Life's Unexpected Moments

Rachael Stewart, LCSW
www.amariscounselingllc.com
rachael@amariscounselingllc.com

Cover Design: Shawn Robinson
727 Marketing: www.727marketingllc.com

ISBN: 979-8-234-16324-0

You're Invited

Life probably won't go according to plan.

That's okay.

This book is an invitation to loosen your grip, enjoy the garden, trust the Gardener, and participate in the beautiful, unfinished work of becoming.

There will be storms.
There will be pruning.
There will be unexpected blooms.

Wherever you are in the journey,
you belong here.

Dedication

To my Mommy Frieda Lynn for the gift of writing and to my Daddy Manzie for always reminding me to use the gift. To my bonus parents Audry, Mama Cynn, and Papa Norm, to whom I owe so much. To Mya, Caleb, and Joshua—being your Mommy is my greatest accomplishment. To Mellow, for all the times my only responsibility was the aux cord. And to my dear friends Joshua Blair and Teria Seah, whose lights were dimmed far too soon. You give me inspiration daily to participate in this beautiful thing called life.

Author's Note

This book is written from my perspective and reflects the meaning I made of my experiences at different stages of my life. Memory is deeply personal, and others who shared these moments may remember them differently. Relationships evolve, and many of the relationships represented in these pages have changed over the years.

As a child, I experienced the world through the understanding I had at the time. As an adult, I have had the privilege of growing in perspective, extending grace, and honoring the complexity of the people who helped shape my story. Today, I hold deep respect, love, and gratitude for my biological, step, and adoptive parents, and I recognize that each has contributed to the woman I have become.

These pages are not written to assign blame or offer a verdict on anyone's character. They are an honest reflection of my lived experience and the lessons I have gathered along the way. This was my experience, and I also recognize that people are more than the hardest chapter I experienced with them.

My hope is that readers will see themselves more than they see the people in my story—that these moments become invitations for reflection, healing, curiosity, and participation in their own unexpected moments.

—*Rachael*

Table of Contents

Introduction

How to Enjoy a Garden Without Becoming the Weather

"I'm fine," I said as I walked into the house of my grieving family. As I cycled through the line of hugs and squeezes, those words kept echoing from my mouth to each family member that asked, "How are you?" Until one of my favorite cousins sat me down and said, "No, you're not. Rachael, your mother just died. It's okay to not be fine." I could feel the release—just a tiny loosening, but the beginning of realizing maybe I didn't have to have it all together.

But as soon as that thought came, another one replaced it—a louder one—"you can handle this."
Because what my cousin didn't see was 9-year-old me getting a pep talk from my dad to "not go in there crying" when we pulled up. She didn't see the fourth grader that had to be clear headed when I found my mom unresponsive and had to page my dad and tend to my 2-year-old brother. She didn't see that as everything I knew to be true disappeared in a matter of minutes; the only thing I had was control. To be strong meant to be in control—of my emotions and how they affected those around me—at least that's what I learned to believe.

That faulty thinking would follow me for many years to come, much more than I am proud of.
The notion that I had to be strong and hold it all together became my identity—so much so that I was given the nickname "Rae of Sunshine," a play on my preferred nickname of Rae.
"You are my sunshine, my only sunshine, you make me happy when skies are gray…"

While that is a sweet, endearing song to many, it became my unofficial theme song. I was even gifted a magnet that hummed that tune and created the "Sunshine dance" to accompany it.

While having a sunny disposition is perfectly healthy, the unhealthy part came when I felt I could never allow myself or others to see the truth—that I existed in the gray as well. I always thought that being Rae of Sunshine meant I had to control the conditions. Which is an easy yet dangerous conclusion to arrive at. Because if I am the hopeful one, the encourager, the one who always has vision or sees possibility, then along the way I also started to believe:

-If things aren't growing, then I should provide more sunlight

-If things aren't blooming, I have to create better conditions

-If there's a struggle, I need to help more

See where I'm going with this?

And then I asked myself one of the most life-changing questions: “Where in my life am I trying to become the weather?” That shifted not just my lens, but my focus. I could now see clearly the years I spent creating the ideal conditions and adjusting myself so that it benefited others. Because that’s what overfunctioning often looks like. Not “I want to control people.” But “I want to create the perfect conditions for growth!” Which sounds noble. Until you’re exhausted.

And so after decades of rehearsing and living out these patterns, I was forced to confront the reality that sunlight had given way to striving. And I paused long enough to finally hear the question God had been asking of me all these years—“What if you don’t have to toil for everything?” Because striving always whispers: “If I can just do enough…” Enough work. Enough helping. Enough carrying. Enough fixing. Then maybe I’ll finally be worthy of rest, love, belonging.

But that is not the value of sunshine. Sunshine isn’t valuable because it eliminates every cloud; it’s valuable because it shines in the middle of ordinary days.

Throughout this journey we will share together, you will hear me reference gardens quite often. And while I am no master gardener and do not have a green thumb, I have always found solace and meaning in the beauty of gardens. If you ask any of my close friends and family, I am always on the hunt for a new botanical garden to visit. It was during one of those visits that God began whispering beautiful truths to me and I learned to do something revolutionary: enjoy the garden, not manage it. Because by finally accepting that He is the Gardener, I am accepting that Someone else is carrying the ultimate responsibility. Someone else is tending roots I can't see. Someone else manages the seasons. Someone else determines growth.

Which means my job changes. Not from important to unimportant. From "I must secure the entire garden" to "I must bloom where I've been planted."

I was no longer led by the thought "I need to inspect, improve, or save the flowers." He just wanted me to become one.

I believe this truth is demonstrated beautifully in His word.

Matthew 6:28–30 says:

"And why are you anxious about clothing? Consider the lilies of the field, how they grow: they neither toil nor spin, yet I tell you, even Solomon in all his glory was not arrayed like one of these. But if God so clothes the grass of the field, which today is alive and tomorrow is thrown into the oven, will he not much more clothe you, O you of little faith?" (ESV)

The Gardener is tending the garden. We get to participate—in the beauty, the storms, the pruning, and the growth. Participation is a skill in itself—it took me years to realize that we all have a little trouble being sons and daughters instead of

Dopplers (always scanning the horizon for the next storm). As both a therapist and an ex-gardener turned flower, I've come to believe that most of us share three familiar companions. I call them the Triplets: Grief, Anxiety, and Potential. They each have a voice. They each promise to keep us safe. And together, they have an uncanny ability to tighten our grip on life until we're so focused on preparing for life we forget to participate in it. You'll meet them throughout these pages.

My goal for this book—in sharing not just my life experiences, but also what I've learned in my career as a therapist—is that if you identify with anything I have said thus far, you begin to realize that life is less about becoming brighter and more about becoming present. Because growth is realizing that sunshine isn't pretending storms don't exist; it's continuing to shine when they do.
So I pray this book gives you the courage to bring your light, but not the entire forecast.

Chapter 1: Control

The Driver's Seat

Have you ever felt like you've always been in the driver's seat of your life? That has been my reality pretty much since childhood. It's like someone handed young Rachael a key and never took it back. Losing my mom at 9 years old, I had to learn so many things so quickly. I mainly learned that life was pretty uncontrollable, which only created a need in me to control it more. To me, if I could control the environment, I could control the outcomes. Insert a very pointed look at the camera. Needless to say, that did not work, and I'm still unlearning some of those patterns even today. I hope that as I share some of these stories as well as some of the tools I've learned along the way, you too can learn to enjoy the ride versus driving all the time.

My first introduction to riding in a car was with my dad. Now, I love him dearly, and I hope he doesn't mind me putting him on blast—but that man drives like a manic Indy 500 driver! He has always had a love for fast cars, and so that often meant that little Rae was in the back seat of a Porsche holding onto her seatbelt for dear life. If I wasn't in the back breathing deeply as we swerved through traffic, I was sitting front row center (literally, thanks to cars of the early 90s with a long middle seat) and would even double as a cup holder for him. Now, I loved spending time with my dad, so these risky car rides often felt worth it. I knew each *Need for Speed* move got us one step closer to any park I desired, and the ride always came with great music. But there also was a lack of control. Because I couldn't say "Dad, slow down" or "Watch out!" without getting a very pointed look and a reminder that he had been driving longer than I've been alive.

Those moments birthed the idea that as soon as I had control of the wheel, I would have control. I could keep myself, and all my passengers, safe as well. Because what is control if not safety? Or so I thought…

In my former marriage, I had a bad habit of always being the one to drive. Sure, I would blame it on motion sickness that I got when riding in the passenger or back seat, but really, it boiled down to my need for control wrapped in cute packaging. See, if I drove, that meant I could not only determine when we left but also when we got there and how fast. I often believed that relationship held so much trust—but of course I could trust the plans—I created them! The hard truth I learned was that it was not trust—it was management. I wasn't safe because my partner was reliable; I felt safe because I had contingency plans.

I realized an important truth: Trust and vulnerability are not always the same. I could trust someone with my life while also not giving them the opportunity to ever show up. This led to such an important question for me, and hopefully one that gives you pause as well: "Can you trust someone without controlling the outcome?" Because love does not issue warranties, it issues invitations. An invitation to trust, to ride, to let someone else navigate.

Fast-forward a few years, and after being divorced and beginning to date again, I now had to wrestle with a nervous system that thrived on control. And so the question was not really "can I trust my partner?" but "can I survive if I am not the one driving?"

And I love the Lord so much because He truly has a sense of humor. The strong-willed recovering control freak, always in the driver's seat, was one day introduced to the world of contingency drivers. If you know anything about those roles, they look a little something like this: show up, adjust to whatever route you're given, and make it work. There are rarely any off days, and "I'm tired" doesn't matter if the load isn't delivered.

How many times had I been contingency driving my own life?

By this point, my résumé of survival had taught me that I had to anticipate every detour and change in the road. Every new season seemed to hand me another reason to keep both hands on the wheel.

Losing my mom taught me life could change in an instant.

Learning to navigate grief, blended families, and competing loyalties taught me to adapt quickly.

Becoming a wife and mother at twenty-one didn't loosen my grip on the wheel. It reinforced my belief that a good wife was competent, capable, and had everything under control. If I didn't know the route, I needed to learn it quickly.

Divorce didn't make me loosen my grip. It made me tighten it.

Then came remarriage. A global pandemic. Parenting a child with autism and ADHD. Being a wife to a partner with autism and depression. Running a private practice while my own life quietly unraveled.

Yet every turn, traffic cone, and detour whispered the same thing: *"Keep driving."*

So I got to the place where not only could I not remember the last time I'd asked someone to drive, I'd accepted driving as an identity and not a choice.

I gritted my teeth, gripped the wheel, and continued managing everyone else's feelings, logistics, and emergencies. And that same little girl who was handed the keys that no one came back for did what she has always done best: drove.

Until recent seasons showed me that maybe I finally get to sit in the passenger seat and just…ride. Now, of course, the driver's seat is never just about you or me. It's about who—or what—is holding the wheel. Sometimes Grief is driving. Sometimes it's Anxiety. Sometimes it's Potential. And while the Triplets are not bad companions, they are terrible backseat drivers—so we often have to gently ask them to move over so we can participate instead of panic.

And it is not always easy to relinquish the wheel. The contingency driver in me loves to keep asking, "Can someone give me a map of the whole journey?" And Life (and the Gardener) keeps answering, "No, but I'll stay in the car with you."

So maybe the lifelong contingency driver doesn't actually need another route. Maybe she needs to discover what it feels like to hand someone else the keys, lean her head against the window, and enjoy the ride.

If you are anything like me, you have spent a lifetime proving you can carry the load. Capability was never the question. Perhaps the terrifying and beautiful question you get to consider now is: "What if you're allowed to be cargo sometimes?"

Changing the Software of Your Nervous System

"If I know I don't have to keep driving…why does it still feel impossible to let go?" This thought is usually followed by "Something must be wrong with me." Let me give you some permission to breathe here. Your nervous system isn't stupid. It's trying to keep you alive; it's just using outdated software.

Our bodies are designed to learn what keeps us safe. That's actually a gift. The problem is that sometimes our nervous system remembers what kept us alive before, even if it no longer serves us now.

While I am the least techy millennial there is, one thing I know is the benefit of a software update. If you try to keep using a smartphone and ignore that update notification, what usually happens? Things slow down, connections often fail, and things that should feel "easy" become a chore. And the thing we delayed because it might take an hour (or 3 hours and 98 minutes, have Apple tell it) is an annoyance we just don't have the time for. Your nervous system isn't broken. It just hasn't realized you're safe enough to install the update. Trust me, if there were a "Remind Me Tomorrow" button for healing the way there is for software updates, I would've clicked it years ago.

Outdated software has a way of narrating your life before you've had a chance to. For example, if you spent your childhood constantly fearing abandonment, critique, or rejection, your nervous system might sound something like this:

They haven't texted back.

- *Old software: "I'm being rejected."*

My boss wants to meet.

- *Old software: "I'm in trouble."*

Someone gives me feedback.

- *Old software: "I'm failing."*

They're moving.

- *Old software: "I'm being left behind."*

They cheated in the past.

- *Old software: "History will repeat itself."*

Your nervous system doesn't ask, "Is this objectively dangerous?" It asks, "Does this feel familiar?" If your body learned that unpredictability meant danger, then a delayed text message, constructive feedback, or someone moving away can feel like a five-alarm fire—even when your thinking brain knows better.

Let's revisit those software examples again with a few updates:

They haven't texted back.

Old software: "I'm being rejected."

New software: "There are at least ten possible explanations, and I only know one of them."

My boss wants to meet.

Old software: "I'm getting fired."

New software: "I don't have enough information yet."

Someone gives me feedback.

Old software: "I failed."

New software: "Feedback isn't a verdict; it's information."

They're moving.

Old software: "I'm being left behind."

New software: "They are including me in their planning."

They cheated in the past.

Old software: "History will repeat itself."

New software: "History is data, not destiny."

Do you see the shift that happens? Recognizing the old software opens the door for compassion. The rules that once protected us can quietly become the very things that keep us stuck. The problem isn't that our nervous system learned the rules. The problem is that it forgot to ask whether those rules still fit. The emergency ended. The rules didn't.

I know. You're probably thinking, "Great...my phone AND my nervous system both need updates now?" Unfortunately...yes. But what that software update does is give us all what we desperately need but rarely get—room to breathe.

I can't tell you how many times I've had the thought, "I know this person isn't my parent, my ex-husband, or my 9-year-old self...so why does my body keep acting like they are?" One of the oldest pieces of software I operated from was "If life gets complicated, become useful." Not because I'm manipulative or a people pleaser. Because somewhere along the way my nervous system learned that usefulness is measurable. Need me to fix it? Need me to carry it? Need me to organize it? Then I was there with a silk-lined Superwoman cape and cute but comfy shoes.

Because usefulness feels safe. Because usefulness can be measured. But what my nervous system had to learn was that I was not in danger of losing someone just because I didn't feel useful at that moment. And so I had to sit quietly with Grief and Anxiety and ask them, “Are we really questioning whether we are lovable, or whether we have to justify our existence here?” My nervous system was trained to see with a lens of usefulness because somewhere inside me there was a little girl who lost people too early and learned that love needed good reasons: good behavior, good performance, good timing, good choices. My nervous system has spent a long time believing that love is demonstrated in emergencies. But this whole season has been teaching something else.

Love lives in logistics. It lives in callbacks. It lives in updates. It lives in shared silence.

I spent so much of my life trying to become unforgettable and useful, and now my nervous system is learning what it feels like to simply be included. But learning that I don’t have to earn my place is one thing. Experiencing what it feels like to actually have a place is another.

For a nervous system that spent years scanning for signs that love could disappear, inclusion can feel surprisingly unfamiliar. It’s one thing to tell yourself, “You belong.” It’s another thing to notice that people have already made room for you—and they aren't waiting for you to prove you deserve the seat.

Maybe healing isn't just learning to stop driving. Maybe it's learning that there is already a seat waiting for you when you do.

Inclusion Is a Form of Love

I have a beautiful biological and stepfamily that I am a part of, and I have also been exceptionally blessed with a chosen adoptive family—an aunt (my mother's sister) and uncle who graciously took me in at age 14 and never looked back. They eventually became my mom and pops, but even then, they were giving me something bigger than a place to live: they were giving me a place to belong.

When I think about that belonging, I fondly think of my pops, who lovingly dove right back into parenting a teenage daughter like he hadn't missed a beat. When I stayed home with cramps, he'd play gospel music for me. I can still remember laughing as he walked out the door, Smokie Norful blasting, and him yelling "God is able, Rachael!"

At the time, it was just my pops being my pops. Looking back, I can see it differently. I wasn't fixing anything. I wasn't carrying anything. I wasn't being useful. I was just being his daughter. I was being cared for. I was being included.

In 2022, my adoptive mom was rushed to the hospital, fighting an illness that blindsided us all. Within the hour, my older sister and I had already taken off work and planned to be on the road to Georgia that evening. As I sat in the hospital the next day, I realized that I wasn't just acting as one of the children anymore. The invitation hadn't changed—my ability to receive it had. And while I know my family would argue that I always have been involved, for me, this moment was so meaningful because I was now being included in healthcare information, aftercare, and how we could all be tangible support. I knew doctors' names, appointment dates, and I could sit in a hospital room during visiting hours reserved for the rotation of children—which I was now a part of. No one had to stop and ask whether I belonged in those conversations. They simply included me. Those aren't grand gestures. They're evidence that someone assumes you'll still be part of tomorrow.

It wasn't the hospital that changed me. It was what the hospital revealed.

This inclusion was transformative because as a child, young Rae was all too familiar with living daily life unseen. After losing my mom, I clung tightly to my dad. Even if the driving was crazy and a bit unpredictable, when he was around, I knew exactly where to sit. The problem was, when he wasn't, I wasn't certain that my seat still existed. I learned to believe that if the driver changed, my place in the car might change too.

As a child, belonging often felt tied to the emotional climate of the house. When my dad left for work, the house became incredibly quiet. Not peaceful, quiet. The kind of quiet where you learn not to take up much space. I could go hours without speaking to anyone except my little brother. With a dad who worked long hours, I was often home with just my stepmom and younger brother, so it was easy to assume I was forgettable because I learned to stay in my room where it felt safer than wondering whether I was welcome in the rest of the house.

That doesn't mean there wasn't love in that house. There was. I can still remember learning my stepmom's recipe for stuffed bell peppers, one of my favorite dishes to this day. But love and belonging are not always experienced the same way, and young Rae didn't yet know how to separate the two. As an adult I can look back and see that love can exist alongside uncertainty, but as a child, I didn't yet have the language to understand the difference. I only knew that sometimes I felt connected, and sometimes I felt like I needed to make myself smaller.

Around age 14, after conflict at home reached a point where I could no longer stay, I found myself in a new home. For a long time I believed I had simply been sent wherever someone had room for me. Years later I learned that wasn't true at all. My mom had already entrusted my aunt and uncle with my care long before I ever needed it. What I experienced as a sudden move from one home to another had, in fact, been an act of intentional love. My nervous system had interpreted survival. Reality had been preparing belonging.

Because belonging once felt like it depended on who was present, my nervous system didn't immediately know what to do with consistent inclusion. It wasn't waiting for another invitation. It was waiting for the invitation to disappear. That's a very different kind of healing.

Over time, these quiet experiences of inclusion kept teaching me something different. My family made room for me. The people who love me keep reminding me I don't have to drive every outcome. And my continued walk with the Gardener keeps whispering the same truth: "I may not know the outcome, but I know who I'm walking with today." That doesn't erase uncertainty. It changes its weight. Not certainty. Inclusion. For someone whose deepest fear has often been being forgotten or left outside the story…ordinary love heals extraordinary fear.

And one of my favorite details: my family includes my twin brothers who are four months younger than me. Because our mothers were pregnant together, we were raised in close proximity, almost like triplets from birth. When my family speaks of us, they lovingly call us triplets. And my aunt and uncle, now my mom and pops, didn't just give me a place to stay. They gave me an identity: one of the triplets.

Not:

"My boys…and Rae."

Not:

"My sons…and my niece."

Just…

The triplets.

That, to me, was the purest form of inclusion.

Because it quietly rewrote my identity.

Being Remembered Is Not the Same as Being Needed

"If I stop earning my place...will people still remember me?"

I know you're probably asking yourself—how many questions does this lady ask herself? A lot. Welcome to my therapist brain where I read myself and others for filth on the regular...

But seriously, I used to think that if I wasn't solving a problem, people might forget I was there. That's not because people were cruel. It's because somewhere along the way I confused being memorable with being necessary.

People don't always remember us because we rescued them. Sometimes they remember us because they felt safe with us. Sometimes they remember us because we chuckled together. Sometimes they remember us because we simply stayed. That is a completely different way of belonging.

To the person who has spent years believing that if they stopped carrying everyone else's load, they'd disappear, accepting my new identities—A Triplet, A Passenger, A Flower in the Garden—didn't make sense because they were less about doing and more about being. So my new challenge involved finding identity after usefulness. Who was I when nobody needed me to save the day?

Being unforgettable is not a reward for being indispensable. In fact, the more indispensable I tried to make myself, the more exhausted I became. And so I had to teach myself that being unforgettable was less about what someone could take from me, and more about the touch I brought. Unforgettable people leave fingerprints.

A fingerprint isn't something you try to leave. It appears naturally when you touch something. As a mother, when I think of fingerprints, I don't think of the cleanup, but of evidence of love that was present. My toddler felt safe enough to steady their hands on a table. The sticky imprint my 6-year-old left on my clothes meant I was the harbor he sought in a rough moment. The makeup-stained prints on the mirror meant my teenage daughter felt comfortable enough to explore her creativity rather than hiding it.

When I first began dating again, I realized that my brain had been trained to do this little accounting trick. I accepted that the other person loved and enjoyed me, but my brain created the caveat, "Well, of course he's remembering me because I bring so much to his life." But what if the actual contribution wasn't an act, but an identity? He was remembering me simply because I was me.

For years I thought my greatest contribution was solving problems. Or that I was a great driver who always knew where I was going. But maybe my greatest contribution was creating spaces where people could simply be themselves. My toddler isn't impressed by my productivity. My 6-year-old isn't evaluating my usefulness. My teenager isn't admiring my accomplishments. They are responding to safety. Presence. Acceptance.

And yes, those make me an excellent driver. But perhaps people weren't holding on because I drove so well. Maybe they stayed because they felt safe riding with me.

Session Summary

This chapter explored how our nervous systems commonly learn to equate control with safety, usefulness with worth, and belonging with performance. Over time, healing invited a different story: one where identity is received rather than earned, and presence matters more than perfection.

Reflection Questions

Question 1: What "rules" have you observed your nervous system creating? Some examples might be:

If people are upset, fix it.

If someone leaves, chase.

If things get uncertain, work harder.

If life gets complicated, become useful.

If I can anticipate it, I can survive it.

Question 2: Reflect on the list of "rules" you observed. Now, I want you to acknowledge and thank your old software for creating these rules to protect you. Then, consider what your new software might be saying.

Question 3: What evidence has your life already given you that challenges one of those old rules?

Treatment Plan

During the upcoming week, begin to notice—not adjust yet, just notice—where you are taking the driver's seat in your life. As you take inventory, notice how your body feels. Is there any tension, racing thoughts, discomfort? Next, imagine opening the driver's side door, walking around the car, and choosing the passenger seat instead. Now notice what your body does. If there is even the slightest shift, it may be worth exploring where you can share or release some responsibilities. I encourage you to find one trusted person—friend, family, or even a therapist—and discuss when you first learned to take the wheel.

Chapter 2: Ownership

When Support Becomes Ownership

As a parent of a child with autism and ADHD, I often found myself giving "disclaimers" for my son's behaviors, moods, etc. While parents often make a list of "things to know" when you have someone babysit, mine went far beyond "eats dinner at 6" or "needs three songs before bed." Mine included things like "needs deep squeezes when he's dysregulated or squish him with a pillow," and "if he starts to hit himself, here's how we deep breathe."
Even as I write this I get a bit emotional because I often carried the weight of how others would experience him, which often led to no support at all. I wasn't just preparing people to care for him—I was trying to manage their experience of him. I wanted them to know he wasn't "bad." I wanted them to understand that there was usually a reason behind his behavior. I hoped that if I explained enough, they would respond with patience instead of judgment. I worried that he wouldn't get invited to sleepovers with the other cousins because people feared how to "manage" him. Looking back, I

wonder if those disclaimers were as much for me as they were for them.

I remember one day recently that really gave me perspective in a tough moment. I had to wait a few hours for my daughter to get out of rehearsal, so I took both my 6-year-old and 2-year-old to a Burger King PlayPlace. Now on any regular day, this can be a lot in itself. But this day, we had to wait until 10 p.m. The playland closed at 9 p.m., my boys were notorious for egging each other on, I had therapy notes I had hoped to finish while they played, **AND** I had PMS. I really felt like I was being punked that day.

I felt myself becoming so overwhelmed and overstimulated that I immediately wanted to cry. Instead, I took a few deep breaths and reached out to one of my trusted friends. She encouraged me to reframe that instead of seeing it as though "My oldest son is choosing chaos," I could say, "Ah, the 7 p.m. version of him has arrived." And now naming the pattern helped me separate the child from the behavior. There are certain times of day when self-control often takes more effort. That doesn't make it less exhausting, but it can make it feel less personal.

Instead of asking, "Why can't I handle this?" I had to try asking, "What was my nervous system carrying today?" One implies failure. The other invites understanding. In that moment, it was not just PMS, two rambunctious kids, and waiting for my teen, but also this underlying feeling that I need to make sure everyone is okay. Because when the meltdowns occur, most times my brain is saying, "I am a bad mom, or I should have prevented this" rather than "What do we all need in this moment?"

I also want to normalize something that parents don't always say out loud. Sometimes the combination—not the individual child—is what tips the scale. We often search for the one thing that's "wrong" when sometimes nothing is wrong at all. Sometimes it's simply that enough manageable things happen at once that they become unmanageable together. I might spend an hour one-on-one with my toddler and have a lovely time. Or one-on-one with my 6-year-old and enjoy his math facts and Minecraft commentary. But together, plus transitions, plus waiting, plus my own hormones? The volume goes up. That's not a reflection on how much I love them, but rather how many inputs my brain is processing simultaneously. How many of us spend the day trying to be everyone else's regulator while having very little regulation flowing back toward us? That doesn't mean anyone is doing something malicious. It means the direction of care is mostly one-way.

So a new train of thought was then created, and the next time he had a meltdown instead of saying, "I have to own this," I can ask, "What is my role?" Because his emotions are his experience, his regulation is a skill he is learning, and my role is to provide safety. Support, not ownership.

Because what I was often doing was taking ownership of his behaviors and outcomes, rather than knowing how to support him. When did I stop advocating for my son...and start apologizing for him? Was I trying to manage his experience...or everyone else's? The more I reflected on it, the more I realized I had been confusing support with ownership in more places than I wanted to admit.

I began noticing it somewhere else—in my relationship with my teenage daughter. My lovingly named "little broke bestie" has unfortunately experienced me wanting to own her responses at times rather than support her in the current transitions. Perhaps if you have a teenager, or can fondly remember being one, you remember the tension between the increase in independence as well as the loss of constant companionship you have with your children when they are younger. There's often a grief that comes with the unpredictability of connecting with a teenager; one moment you're belting out Hamilton lyrics in the car and the next they are giving you noncommittal shrugs and grunts. But often that loss can come from a feeling of losing ownership of the way the relationship feels. And ownership for most of us makes us feel needed and wanted, which we then equate with connection.

Have you ever confused being needed with being loved? But children don't stop being connected to us when they stop needing us in the same way. Support is realizing that the achievement and the ache can arrive together. I can celebrate my daughter becoming more independent while grieving that she doesn't need me in quite the same way. Those emotions aren't competitors—they're companions.

Parenting might ask us to hold pride and sadness together. Mutuality isn't something you demand from your children. It's something you learn to appreciate when it naturally emerges—and something you grieve, a little, when adolescence makes it less predictable.

But the pattern didn't stop with parenting. I began to notice it in my second marriage, too. I picked up many of the mental loads because I believed that he wouldn't. I became not just the manager of our calendar, but eventually the manager of every person in the household. I scheduled appointments, initiated conversations, and became the driving force behind our family operations. One instance I recall vividly was a time during couples therapy when I was feeling at the edge of exhaustion. I remember sitting not with tears but numbness, recalling every way I had managed the family and family members that week. I felt how shallow I was breathing. I can still feel how even though we sat next to each other, the chasm between me and my ex-husband was filled with incomplete tasks and unexpressed expectations. I remember looking at my therapist and my ex-husband and just saying three words that had become not just a prayer but an SOS call—**I need help.** I remember feeling the weight of the world and that if I didn't do it, it wouldn't happen. Every time I tested whether someone else would carry the responsibility, the experiment seemed to confirm my fear. When I tried to release it, the experiment resulted in unwashed laundry, prescriptions forgotten to be picked up, and an ever-piling to-do list that went unacknowledged. So I became my own answer and embodied the help I was asking for.

I thought that because I loved helping—and because it made me feel needed, competent, and in control—helping was the answer. The switch from helping to managing was so silent that I didn't fully recognize it until I was the one screaming. It didn't happen overnight. There was no celebration or cake that announced, "Congrats, you've been promoted from helper to manager." It happened one small decision at a time, until doing everything was just…normal.

And I won't lie, perhaps the scariest part was the conversation with myself I avoided having. What did control not only cost me but give me? Because some things we do, not just because they work, but because they also feel good. That's the uncomfortable part of ownership. Sometimes we don't keep carrying everything because no one else will but because we have become very good at carrying everything. And being good at something can quietly become part of your identity.

Sometimes there's a quiet pride in thinking, *I'm just better at this,* so I keep doing the whole budget. I knew everyone's medication schedule without looking. I knew which bills were due. I knew what was running low before it ever made it to the whiteboard. I wore that competence like a badge that only seemed to encourage my new role of Household Manager. Having my partner tell me "Your ideas are always good, so that's why I go with them" can feel like a compliment in your wisdom bucket, even if you are tired of planning. It sounded like trust. But somewhere along the way, I interpreted it as an assignment. Sometimes there's a quiet satisfaction in becoming the person everyone relies on. At first, it feels like appreciation. Eventually, it becomes an expectation, which then leads to exhaustion.

After divorce and in coparenting I've now had to continue practicing the same lessons—support isn't control. I can stay connected to my kids without taking over every piece of the response. And that is not saying, "Everything is fine," but rather, "I'm going to behave in a way that leaves room for a different outcome."

Getting out of rescuing doesn't mean ignoring legitimate concerns. The thought doesn't have to be "They are always capable," but "I'm going to let capability be tested before I assume incapability." My old instinct was to rescue, but now growth was prompting me to not add a new responsibility but instead remove one that no longer belonged to me.

Every time I ask, "Whose responsibility is this?" I'm not looking for someone to blame. I'm looking for the place where love can finally breathe again. I'm asking myself: Can I honor what I see without becoming responsible for what they choose? I am accepting that I don't have to feel responsible for making sure a situation or person becomes the picture that I all too often can see in advance. Because there is a subtle but powerful difference between nurturing the possibility and guaranteeing an outcome. One is influence and the other is ownership. And ownership is heavy when the puzzle pieces belong to someone else.

Seeing the Puzzle Doesn't Give You Ownership of the Pieces

Imagine you're standing over a puzzle and you can clearly see the picture on the box. You know where the pieces should go. You know what it could become. But the pieces are in someone else's hands. You can point to the picture, encourage them, sit beside them, and even celebrate progress. But you cannot choose for them to assemble it. And if you grab all the pieces and start building it yourself, eventually one of two things happens: 1. You become exhausted. 2. They never develop ownership of the picture.

Many of us have a genuine gift for seeing the picture before the puzzle is finished. We see strengths before they are obvious, growth before it arrives, and possibilities before they are visible. While that is truly beautiful, it also creates a challenge in which we can become emotionally invested in a future that someone else has not yet chosen.

As a therapist, this is something that happens quite often and can make it feel like my brain is playing chess while everyone else sees a checkerboard. But instead of knights and rooks, I naturally see patterns, attachment dynamics, communication problems, and trauma responses. The problem was that my therapist brain didn't know how to clock out. The chessboard came home with me, and so did the DSM!

My underlying software has always been "If I can predict it, surely I'm supposed to prevent it." This is where some of my favorite characters entered: Grief, Anxiety, and Potential.

Anxiety told me to prevent while Potential told me to predict. Grief whispered that she could stay away if I prepared for every possible outcome. Not because I wanted control for control's sake. Because uncertainty felt expensive. My Triplets never shout "We like control!" No, they stand tall with a mixture of fear and hope in their eyes, asking me, "If we prepare enough, can we protect the people we love?"

I remember early in one relationship there was an instance when my partner was making a pretty big decision about where to be geographically. Immediately, I could map everything out. Housing. Kids. Distance. Finances. Timeline. Future. And child, let me tell you there's not a puzzle that Rae does not get excited about. I opened Zillow, I mentally rearranged custody schedules, I imagined how our kids would get along and which school districts might support us best. My brain built the entire puzzle in about thirty seconds. But what actually belonged to me? My piece was simply: "Can I be present while he decides?" That was a huge realization. Insight is not ownership. Sometimes wisdom says, "I see exactly what's happening" without adding, "Therefore I must intervene."

And remember that old software we talked about? Mine was screaming that if I couldn't help him figure it out, I wasn't being useful, and therefore I wasn't needed. And, if I zoom out, I think the deeper belief I was healing from sounded something like this:

"If I can see the need, maybe God showed it to me because I'm supposed to meet it."

And what I slowly learned was this: Sometimes God lets me see something so I can have compassion, so I can pray, so I can understand, so I can witness, or simply love someone without trying to become their solution. Seeing was never automatically synonymous with solving.

This is why the distinction between what is revealed to you and what is assigned to you is so critical. I often would work from the algorithm, "something is revealed to me, therefore it must be my assignment." But sometimes a thing is revealed for me to appreciate, but not carry. I spent years believing that seeing the picture meant I had to carry the pieces. Now I know those are different gifts. Maybe you've been confusing them too. Seeing the picture is a gift. Carrying all the pieces is not a requirement. Looking back, I realized I had been working a job I was never hired to do.

Stop Applying for Positions That Were Never Posted

What imaginary jobs have you accepted? If you are anything like me, your resume may include:

Director of Everyone Else's Emotional Regulation

Vice President of Preventing Natural Consequences

Chief Officer of Future Outcomes

Manager of Other People's Potential

Executive Coordinator of Things God Never Asked Me to Coordinate

Holy Spirit Jr.

Once I accepted that these were positions I was never meant to hold, I truly believe Heaven's HR first action item was to send me this loving little memo.

INTERNAL MEMO

To: Rae

From: Heaven's Human Resources

Subject: Position Clarification

Dear Rae,

After reviewing your current responsibilities, we've noticed you've accepted several positions that were never assigned to you.

Effective immediately, you are no longer authorized to:

- Become the weather
- Carry all the puzzle pieces
- Accept every referral
- Force flowers to bloom
- Manage the entire ecosystem

Thank you for your cooperation. Your replacement has already been arranged. (And yes, they already know where the office is.)

Imagine my surprise when I sat still and realized that not only did I invent the jobs, but I had also written the job descriptions. But I never once stopped to ask who hired me, what I was still trying to prove, or, more importantly, what happens when I resign?

The Gardener position was filled. The Weather position was filled. The Savior position was filled. Heaven's HR has confirmed there are no current openings. That's when I could finally accept a new thought: If I don't do it, that's okay. God has never been short-staffed. Not because I don't care or it doesn't matter. But because the world was functioning long before I arrived and will continue long after I leave.

God has other employees. The Garden already has a Gardener. The weather does not rely on me.

The Garden Has a Gardener and It's Not Me

What if the opposite of trying to be the Gardener isn't becoming just a visitor to the garden, but allowing yourself to become part of it?

It's finally allowing yourself to become one of the flowers. Flowers don't wake up wondering whether they're producing enough petals. They don't compare blooms or panic when another flower blossoms first. They don't strategize how to make spring come sooner. They simply receive, remain, respond to the sun, and grow.

As I stated before, I am nobody's horticulturist and the only reason my current houseplant is still living is because my dad rescued it from my living room and put it on life support on his front porch. But my lack of a green thumb did teach me some important lessons, such as you can overwater something because you care too much. And that plants recover best after you stop fussing with them.

Every time I visit a botanical garden, something in me slows down before I even realize it has happened. I find myself noticing that my pace changes, my breathing gets deeper, my shoulders unclench and my smile gets just a bit wider. I don't think I've ever left one feeling hurried. I marvel at how effortlessly the flowers embody their identity. They embrace who they were created to be without ever having to be taught. No rose is trying to become lavender. The sunflowers don't apologize for being too tall. Everything just grows because it's connected to its source.

The older I get, the more fascinated I become by gardeners. I marvel at the patience my dad has when he is puttering around his garden—whether in silence or with his portable speaker blasting oldies. He wanders with an unrushed pace and will often just sit for hours accompanying his plants. Gardeners don't stand over flowers yelling or pull fruit out of the branches. They cultivate, prune, water, and wait. And in that waiting, that silence, that enjoying the weather instead of being it—I think we as flowers get clarity.

Who am I once I stop trying to be everything else? I've realized that I've always just been one of the flowers, loved by the Gardener long before I ever tried to become Him. One thing about flowers is that they never question whether the Gardener notices them. They don't perform for the Gardener, but they simply bloom because they're alive.

Once I stopped trying to become the Gardener, I realized the questions themselves had changed. Maybe that's what healing does. It doesn't always give us all the answers. Sometimes it simply teaches us to ask better questions. What gardens have I wandered into because I confused love with responsibility? What flowers have I been pulling open before their season?

And what might finally grow in my own life if I trusted the Gardener more than my ability to manage the garden?

Session Summary

This chapter explored how we often confuse what is revealed to us with what actually belongs to us. As you reflected, I hope you noticed that the deeper question was never simply, "What am I doing?" but "**Who am I** when I'm no longer doing all of those things?" These reflections don't invite us to become less responsible; they invite us to become rightly responsible.

Reflection Questions

Question 1: Where have you mistaken ownership for love?

Question 2: What "job titles" have you quietly given yourself over the years? If Heaven's HR wrote you a memo today, what positions would you be asked to resign from?

Question 3: In what relationships or environments is it easiest for you to simply be a flower—receiving, remaining, and growing? Where is it hardest to trust the Gardener?

Question 4: What responsibility would you lay down today if you truly believed the Gardener had not forgotten your garden?

Treatment Plan

Take a blank page. Across the top write: **"Things I Thought Were My Responsibility"**

Then don't censor yourself. Write everything that comes to mind.

Examples: Keeping peace. Explaining my child. Fixing my marriage. Making sure everyone liked me. Preventing conflict. Making holidays perfect.

After your list is complete, create two columns titled: Mine to Carry and The Gardener's. Slowly move each responsibility into the column where it truly belongs. As you finish, notice what emotions come up when you move something from your column to the Gardener's. Do you notice relief? Fear? Resistance? Hope? Those emotions are part of the work too.

Chapter 3: Security

Outcome Security Versus Relational Security

You know something my nervous system LOVES? Security (no surprise there, right?) And one of the things I've discovered is the difference between outcome security and relational security. In past seasons, outcome security was my favorite because it says "I know exactly what's going to happen." But relational security says "I know I'll be brought into the conversation as things unfold." That is often much more durable because outcomes change; people lose jobs, moves fall through, cars break down, kids get sick. Life...lifes. But relational security often looks like a conversation that says "Here's what changed." And that creates a different type of stability, not of certainty but of partnership.

Outcome security asks, "Can I know how the story ends?" Relational security asks, "Do I trust the person reading the next chapter with me?" We often don't realize which kind of security we're pursuing until life refuses to cooperate with our plans.

When I think back on my first marriage, I wasn't primarily choosing a husband. I was choosing a home. As a young woman who had lost her mother at 9, I wasn't looking just for romance, but belonging. Security seemed to offer me permanence, and that felt safe. By my second marriage, I wasn't looking for permanence anymore. I was looking for predictability. If I know exactly how things will pan out and when, then I must be safe. If someone asked me to name each season of my life, I think it would sound something like this:

Chapter 1 (Marriage 1): Hold the Dream Tightly

Chapter 2 (Marriage 2): Hold the Timeline Tightly

Chapter 3 (Post-Divorce): Hold the Potential Lightly

Current Chapter: Hold Hope Closely and Expectations Loosely

It's funny how every season thought it had finally found the answer. In reality, every season was searching for the same thing. I just kept changing where I searched. At first I looked for it in permanence. Then I looked for it in plans. Then I looked for it in potential. I wasn't actually chasing different things. I was chasing the same feeling—safety. Only now do I realize I had been looking for it in places that couldn't consistently provide it. The answer wasn't certainty; it was presence.

That realization changed more than my relationships with people. It quietly changed how I understood my relationship with God, too. When I zoom out, I can see the same lesson appearing in other places. In a relationship, I may be learning I don't have tomorrow's blueprint, but I haven't been left out of the journey. With God, I discovered something even steadier. I still don't have tomorrow's blueprint, but I know the One who walks with me.

Different relationships, same invitation. Not certainty but presence. One of these builds safety from the circumstances, while the other builds safety from relationships.

It is also fair to acknowledge that not everyone has trustworthy relationships right now. Friend, if that's where you are, I'm really glad you're still reading. That reality doesn't make you cynical. It makes you someone who's been hurt. One of the hardest parts about healing is that we often need relationships to recover from relational wounds. Trust me, there have been many days I've thought, "I could heal a lot easier and faster if people just weren't involved!" That's deeply unfair, and yet it's often how healing unfolds. One of the things Scripture has slowly taught me is that God rarely begins by explaining everything that's about to happen. More often, He begins by reminding people that He is with them.

Once I started noticing that pattern, I couldn't unsee it. Again and again, when people in Scripture faced uncertainty, God's first response wasn't usually to hand them a detailed plan. It was to remind them of His presence.

***Joshua hears: "Be strong and courageous...for the Lord your God will be with you wherever you go"* (Joshua 1:9, NIV)**

***Isaiah is reminded: "When you pass through the waters, I will be with you"* (Isaiah 43:2, NIV)**

***Jesus encourages His disciples: "I am with you always"* (Matthew 28:20, NIV)**

The promise isn't usually, "Nothing difficult is coming." It's, "You won't face it alone." God's presence doesn't eliminate our need for people. In many ways, it teaches us what trustworthy presence looks like, so we can recognize it, receive it, and eventually offer it to others.

Security isn't always knowing what tomorrow will bring. Sometimes it's knowing you won't have to discover tomorrow alone. Looking back, I don't think I was chasing certainty because I loved having a plan. I was chasing certainty because I thought it was the only way to feel safe. It turns out safety was never something certainty could give me. It was something presence had been offering all along.

What Sustains Us

My nervous system thought stability looked like certainty. Certainty was the only safety it knew. Imagine 9-year-old Rachael: "If I know what happens, life can't catch me off guard." And then again at 30, "If I know exactly what my partner will do and when, I won't be hurt." Seasons of life seemed to reinforce: If I know the plan, I can prepare. If I prepare, I can adapt. But did that certainty actually protect me? My old software computed that knowing what happens creates safety. The new software and experience suggest that who it's happening with actually creates safety.

My heart is learning stability is actually faithful presence. It's grandparents taking my boys to the park when I'm overstimulated. It's a maturing mother-daughter relationship that lets a teenager hug you in a vulnerable moment. It's friends who send a text after you've had a rough week. It's a partner who stays on FaceTime while you're trying to get a toddler to sleep.

For so long, safety drove me towards certainty, and then finally, after one too many storms shook my foundation, I heard "Safety comes from not being abandoned in collapse."

And I realized that certainty never actually protected me. PRESENCE did. My parents. My siblings. My children. My partner. My friends. I have spent a lifetime trying to guarantee that I would not be abandoned when the Gardener was asking me to let myself notice that I am already accompanied.

And again, friend, if you're anything like me, you have spent more nights than you can count yelling at Heaven with tears of frustration in your eyes, saying, "Why can't I just accept this? The love, the presence?" And if I can lean in and hold your hand a minute, I want to answer that.

Because acceptance is not the opposite of fear; acceptance is the opposite of control. You can absolutely accept being loved and still be scared. You can absolutely trust someone and still have old software running in the background. You can absolutely be healing and still have Triplet activation.

Now don't laugh, but I have "committee meetings" with myself all the time. And the conversations oscillate between tears, laughter, and my inner therapist and Holy Spirit reading me for filth some days. But these meetings are often where I have confronted some of my deepest fears. I've had uncomfortable conversations about how eventually everyone will leave because I'm too much. That if I ask for less, maybe they'll stay. Because somewhere along the way, the fear of expressing a need became more painful than whatever the answer might be. (Ouch, right? At least my personal sessions come with a blanket and good snacks.)

Healing isn't "I never get scared again." Healing is "I notice I'm scared and I don't let fear drive."

What if accepting love feels irresponsible because vigilance kept you safe? Because if you're relaxed, or too hopeful, or stop planning, you could get hurt. But stability isn't always fixed circumstances. Many times, it shows up when a reliable person is present in our changing circumstances.

And I know you're sitting there with a side-eye because what I'm describing sounds suspiciously like TRUST. But I wonder if it's actually this: we all have been waiting for permission to rest. Too often,

I have found myself saying, “If I had a timeline I could just breathe.” Knowledge of when a hard season would end. Or when something exciting would happen. Or when I could get to that special destination that would somehow be “safer” because it was known.

I imagine myself at so many different ages, with wide eyes and trembling hands holding a map, asking myself over and over, “What do we do if we don’t know where we are going?” And the Gardener keeps kneeling next to me, not trying to take the map, but simply whispering, “Rae, you can breathe now. I’m with you.”

Safety wasn’t the question.

Surrender wasn’t the question.

Sustenance was.

Remaining

I have spent a lot of time thinking about the things that last. Experiencing a major loss at such a young age taught me that things are temporal, so my perspective has always been shaped through the lens of legacy. If I leave this earth at 44 or 104, what have I accomplished? What impact did I leave? Who felt the weight of my presence? So much of my mother's memory lives on because I share what her presence meant to me—from indoor picnics in the rain to the patience it took to play Barbies for hours at a time.

Presence often had very little to do with where we were going, but everything to do with the fact that we were together. I knew that with her I found safety, comfort, and friendship. And apart from her, I was left to figure out who and what was safe. When I think about my own children, no matter whether it's my 15-year-old daughter, 6-year-old son, or 2-year-old son, when they are hurt, the response is almost always the same—"Come here." Before I know what happened, whose fault it was, or decide what needs to be fixed, I want them close. I may ask later for them to tell me what happened, but the initial answer is my presence, not my problem-solving. Presence comes before explanation.

Maybe that's why Jesus' invitation in John 15 has always felt so familiar to me.

John 15:1–5 says:

"I am the true vine, and my Father is the gardener. He cuts off every branch in me that bears no fruit, while every branch that does bear fruit he prunes so that it will be even more fruitful. You are already clean because of the word I have spoken to you. Remain in me, as I also remain in you. No branch can bear fruit by itself; it must remain in the vine. Neither can you bear fruit unless you remain in me. I am the vine; you are the branches. If you remain in me and I in you, you will bear much fruit; apart from me you can do nothing" (NIV).

Maybe "Remain" is simply God's version of saying, "Come here."

What is your answer when He calls? Mine used to be: Give me a minute. Let me see if I can fix it first. If I understand it better, maybe I can comfort myself—no need to bother You.

For years I read "remain" as another assignment. Another spiritual discipline I needed to get better at. If I stayed close enough, prayed enough, trusted enough, maybe then I'd finally experience peace. It never occurred to me that Jesus wasn't giving me another performance metric. He was offering companionship.

Jesus doesn't say, "I will explain every season before it comes." He doesn't say, "I'll give you the five-year plan." He says, "Remain." Why? Because remaining answers a different question. Not, "What will happen?" But, "Who will sustain you?" Presence changes response. Not prediction.

We often confuse prediction with discernment. Discernment is often taught as learning to anticipate what is coming next. But discernment isn't asking, "What future am I trying to predict?" It's asking, "Whose presence am I counting on while I walk into it?" Not because the future suddenly became predictable. But because, day by day, week by week, season by season, you start discovering something you've never really trusted before. That you don't have to survive the future alone. Whether it's with the Gardener or whether it's with the people He's placed around you.

I learned rest is the language that presence teaches us. For so many, myself included, rest was something to be earned, not something implied. I wore my exhaustion as evidence I was doing enough. I can remember so many holidays, events, even a regular Tuesday when I overextended myself with just one more email, one more calendar opening, one more check-in on a friend—not that these weren't good things, but they shifted my focus more toward projects than presence.

But remaining taught me something different. Fruitfulness came from closeness, not calendars. Rest wasn't the reward for finishing the work. It became the evidence that I trusted the Gardener with what remained unfinished.

I can recall many nights a few years ago, when I sat in the bathroom at 2 a.m. weeping, hands raised with more questions than words I could utter. I was exhausted from trying to figure out how to "save" a failing marriage, sustain two kids, and carry another through all the uncertainty. The unfinished seemed loud, and I kept feeling like ***doing*** was the answer to quiet the noise. I scheduled more therapy appointments, planned date nights, researched and intellectualized, until finally the only thing that was left was hearing the invitation and finally looking up—"Come here." Some days I dragged myself and some days I ran, but I finally said yes.

I had mistaken activity for abiding and had been trying to produce on my own what only proximity could create. I don't expect my children to have all the answers before they climb into my arms. Why did I assume God expected that from me? I can see that "remain" was never another assignment. It has always been His way of saying,

"Come here."

Session Summary

This chapter reminded us that security isn't something we manufacture through control. It's something we experience through faithful presence. We explored where we've been looking for security, what actually sustains us, and what it means to remain.

Reflection Questions

Question 1: Where have you said to yourself, "If I had a timeline, I could just breathe?"

Question 2: What has given you security in the past?

Question 3: Where do you experience faithful presence most in your life right now? In your relationship with God? In your community? In your closest relationships? As you reflect, notice what faithful presence feels like in your body.

Treatment Plan

Take some time this week to sit with Jesus' invitation to "Come here." What do you feel when you hear those words? What is currently making it difficult to say yes?

Chapter 4: Participation

From Preparation to Participation

If remaining taught me where my life is sustained, participation asks me what I do with the life I'm actually living. Remaining asked me to practice a kind of stillness that didn't seem to fit my expectations of growth. I thought growth should look like movement.

What if stillness isn't the absence of movement, but movement in a different direction? Not outward, but downward. Roots grow in stillness, even when the flower they're anchoring looks inactive from above. An entire system can be developing beneath the surface while, from above, it looks like nothing is happening. So the focus becomes not doing more, but being willing to participate in the growth that's already happening.

If I'm honest, I was often stuck in a subtle trap: "If I can just prepare enough...then I'll finally be ready to live." Except the finish line kept moving. I would prepare, then prepare for the next thing. Then optimize, organize, research. Somewhere along the way, preparation quietly became avoidance—not because I was afraid of the work, but because preparation felt safer than participation. Preparation had served me well, but eventually additional preparation was no longer readiness. It was delay.

After two divorces, participating in love and life often felt reckless. I felt that even with the best preparation, I had somehow still failed, and preparing more would be the only way to "win." To sit in the vulnerability of being sought after again, to hope that I—with all my "baggage"—could be an answer was terrifying. And there was the wound: I was trying to be an answer instead of an occupant. I was stuck in fix-it mode instead of enjoying what I had quietly been building on my own.

My future had less to do with what I lost in the past and much more to do with the rebuilding that happened after the storms. Though a significant relationship was lost, my identity, family, friendships, career, and even my capacity to love were still mine.

I was learning the difference between putting something on my calendar and actually being in the parking lot about to walk through the door. Planning had always felt productive. Participation required me to actually show up.

I can remember a simple, ordinary day that taught me the beauty of truly participating. My boyfriend at the time called me while I was at the gym, and I missed the call. Thanks to what I'm convinced is Planet Fitness's terrible Wi-Fi and my nervous system conspiring against me, I began overthinking why he hadn't responded to a message I sent. Later, while talking, he casually mentioned that he'd called because he'd tried a Dunkin' Refresher and wanted to tell me about it. When I eventually looked at the timeline, I saw that the notification hadn't come through until hours after he'd actually called. I realized the evidence I was using to build a story wasn't even the whole story.

Old Rachael could have gone:

> "He's being distant."
>
> "He's not thinking about me."
>
> "Something feels different."
>
> "I need to figure out what's happening."

Three chapters ahead.

Current Rachael was able to go:

> "Oh. I missed the call."
>
> "He was actually trying to tell me about his day."
>
> "Okay. Let me update the story."

Sometimes staying present can save a relationship. It can also save you from having a conversation with a problem that doesn't actually exist. There was another layer I could have gotten stuck in. I could have worried that he would be upset with me for mentioning his lack of response when I had missed his call myself. Instead, he extended grace. Another piece of evidence that I didn't have to turn every misunderstanding into a problem that needed to be solved. I was learning to become curious before becoming convinced. And that's when I realized how often my Triplets were doing something similar: taking incomplete information and preparing me for a loss that hadn't actually happened.

The subtle belief underneath over-preparing is: "I need to do something right now or I might lose something." In that moment at the gym, there was nothing I needed to fix. I needed more information. I needed to stay present long enough for the rest of the story to arrive.

And once again, I could almost see the Triplets sitting around the conference table. Grief, Anxiety, and Potential. Blueprints spread across the table, a PowerPoint slide deck primed and ready to go. Politely, in turn, each would speak their piece:

Grief: *"Remember what happened last time."*

Anxiety: *"Then let's make sure it doesn't happen again."*

Potential: *"And here's every possible way it could happen."*

Together, they made me incredibly good at preparing for a life I hadn't actually stopped to inhabit.

Grief doesn't need to be diminished. She has helped me survive enormous things. She knows exactly what it costs to lose something, so she is always looking for the next thing that might disappear.

Anxiety had me wondering for years if the house was actually secure or if I had simply missed something in the blueprint. Friend, it's like going to HomeGoods and buying all this beautiful stuff but never actually unpacking it because you're worried you're going to get evicted. I became more practiced at prepping for loss than inhabiting security. I spent so much energy making sure the house would survive that I forgot I was allowed to live in it.

And then there is Potential, who can see what everything could become. Potential is beautiful. She gives us hope. A relationship could become something. A person could grow. A project could flourish. But potential is an invitation, not a guarantee. Reality is evidence.

The deeper question was: Can I trust that I am ready enough to participate in what is already here? The opposite of preparation isn't recklessness—it's participation.

Old Rachael was always reading ahead. I'd be halfway through the ending before the scene had finished happening. Current Rachael is learning to put the book down. Not because I don't care how the story ends, but because I finally understand I can't experience a chapter while I'm busy predicting the next one.

Hope Without a Stopwatch

What happens when the life I want isn't here yet? If we're being honest, we've all been ready to skip right to the finale or read the CliffsNotes. We seek out the TL;DR version instead of absorbing all the details.

But what do we believe we'll gain by knowing the ending? Peace? Clarity? Control? For me, it was often all three. Somehow I believed knowing what was coming would make the present easier to live in. I confused wanting hope with having a deadline.

In so many ways, I was rushing through experiences because I was already mentally standing at the next milestone. We all do it. We forget to celebrate losing the first 10 pounds because we're already preparing for 20. We can't wait to get to graduation, forgetting that we just got all As. We start mentally planning Pinterest-worthy weddings and neglect to celebrate that we're finally in a healthy, safe relationship. None of these things are bad. But when we're always focused on what something will become, we can miss what it already is.

Timelines have always been a bit of a love language to me. I don't just love knowing how I'm getting somewhere, but when. I've carried deadlines not always because I wanted something, but because I had something to prove. Whether it was proving I was mature enough to get married and start a family, or that I'd achieved "successful" singleness long enough to be ready to remarry, meeting a deadline somehow became synonymous with my capability.

When the timelines didn't keep tempo with my actual life, I often confused waiting with being stuck. I began using hope as a measurement of whether my life was progressing correctly, rather than something that accompanied me on the journey. And if I sit with myself for a minute, I realize I was waiting to feel something once the "thing" happened—a new job, a better schedule, a new relationship, a new experience. The feeling I was waiting for was often relief, as if I were holding my breath while approaching my destination.

Many of my life plans were formed around the question, “Where is this going?” When would a relationship get serious? When would I reach the next plateau of ambition? When would I see progress in the people I love? And while I lived in the tension of the not yet, a new question began to emerge: Maybe the question isn’t where I’m going, but who I—and the people around me—are becoming along the way. In past relationships, I was often focused on the next step rather than watching us both become our truest selves.

Those are radically different experiences. One is timeline-focused. The other is person-focused.
That shift forced me to realize that my expectations weren’t actually based on the current relationship. They were inherited from previous relationships, cultural expectations, and social media.

The greatest gift I’ve received from a partner was learning that “not yet” doesn’t automatically mean "no." A delay isn't evidence that something won't happen; sometimes "not yet" is simply a different timeline, not a different outcome. Which, in theory, I should have understood because I tell my children this all the time. If I know they have sprinkles and fun toppings waiting for them at home, telling them not to eat the ice cream in the car isn't punishment. It's patience. The promise of the ice cream hasn't disappeared just because they have to wait until they get home. A child can experience "not yet" as deprivation. A secure person can experience "not yet" as information.

And this concept is not just for relationships, but everyday life. The difference between hope and expectation, to me, is this: Hope says, "I'm excited for this to happen." Expectation says, "I'm waiting for this to happen." Hope lets me enjoy the journey. A deadline makes me evaluate it. Hope asks us to genuinely want something without deciding that God, or a person, or life owes it to us by a certain date. The answer isn't pretending you don't care. It's learning to hope without turning hope into a stopwatch.

I remember shortly after divorce I had this feeling like I was waiting for something. Being so used to domestic life, I yearned for companionship and things "getting back to normal." I spent months trying to recreate the same rhythms and figure out what could be added to my life, until my own therapist reminded me that contentment wasn't about having a busy life, but a full one. I realized that the things I hoped for weren't just found in marriage, but in my kids, community, hobbies, and even in my alone time. I looked up and realized, "Wait, I'm actually enjoying this. I'm not waiting for my real life to begin. This is my life."

During some of the hardest seasons of my life, I realized I was expecting God to be on a timeline. I unconsciously assumed there was a sequence He was supposed to follow because the answer meant something like this: He heard me; I made the right decision; I was finally on track; my life could be normal again; or, even bigger, my suffering had been worth it.

I can want something deeply without making its timing the evidence of whether God is faithful, whether my life is working, or whether I'm on the right path. I knew this as head knowledge, but my heart often fought against it. If God wasn't answering yet, I wondered whether I had misunderstood, made the wrong choice, or wasn't where I was supposed to be. I convinced myself that the delay itself was evidence that something was wrong.

Friend, can I be really honest? There is so much sadness when things don't happen how you expect. I've not only counseled others through these seasons; I've lived through them myself when the timeline seemed to evade me. I hoped healing would come sooner, but instead, I lost a dear friend. I hoped that I'd see my partner more, but distance kept getting in the way. I hoped that I would buy a home, or find a new community, and each day passed without my dreams being realized.

And it's okay to grieve when the deadline disappoints you. The issue isn't that you had a timeline. The issue is believing that a timeline is a promise. Those are different. Grief doesn't always mean you're on the wrong path. Sometimes it simply means the path is taking longer than your heart hoped.

And trust me, I get it when you're waiting for something your heart deeply desires. Many of us aren't rushing simply because we're impatient. It's the wound beneath the deadline that says, "If this doesn't happen soon enough, it means it isn't going to happen at all." We hear that voice when we're waiting for marriage or remarriage, hoping for a pregnancy, waiting for healing during an illness, or wondering when a difficult season of parenting will finally feel easier. The circumstances may be different, but the question underneath them can be the same: *How long do I have to wait before I can believe things are going to be okay?* Wanting those things does not require you to treat today as an incomplete version of your life, just an unopened one.

I don't need a deadline in order for hope to be legitimate. When I try to stop negotiating the timing, my relationship with God gets freer. And I learn to enjoy my life instead of evaluating it. But once I stopped evaluating whether my life was on schedule, I realized I was still evaluating something else: myself.

Being Enjoyed Instead of Evaluated

Picture this: We enter a beautiful botanical garden. There's an archway filled with fragrant flowers—gardenia, lilac, jasmine, and roses. You take a deep inhale and feel the sun warming your skin. You notice a bench facing the water, sit down, and allow the breeze to wash over you.

As you settle into the scene, notice your thoughts. Are you asking the flowers to bloom a certain way or the water to change its pace? Or is simply being in the space enough to invite curiosity rather than critique?

Sitting in that garden, I realized how often I approached my own life differently. I wasn't simply experiencing it. I was evaluating it. Was I doing enough? Was I growing enough? Was I where I should be? Being evaluated made me feel pressured to perform. Evaluation became, "How do I make this garden what it should be?" Enjoyment asked, "How do I relax here?"

When life got complicated, my instinct was to ask what I could contribute. Somewhere underneath that instinct was the belief that my value depended on my usefulness. I had started treating love like it came with a scorecard. When you're stuck in an evaluation mindset, even a good relationship can become an assessment: Am I communicating correctly? Am I being supportive enough? Am I reacting appropriately? Am I lovable enough?

Usefulness feels earned; enjoyment is received. Enjoyment doesn't mean everything feels good. It means I can experience something without immediately asking what it says about me.

I wasn't just asking whether I was worthy. I was asking whether I could stop performing long enough to receive what was already being offered.

And as a therapist, I'd dare say I'm even harder on myself. I can't remember how many times I've said to myself and others, "I should know this. I teach it every day." As if my master's degree had somehow exempted me from having an attachment style or needing to regulate. I'd spend far too long rereading a text or overthinking a response, withholding a genuine feeling because I was afraid of how it would be received. I was so focused on protecting the other person's experience that I stopped paying attention to my own. Typing and deleting a text. Hesitating to ask something outright in case it would be an inconvenience. I was learning that attention and interpretation are not the same thing. Something could get my attention without immediately becoming a verdict about me. These patterns revealed that I wasn't just asking whether I was loved. I was asking whether I was a good enough experience for someone else.

But allowing myself to be known, enjoyed, and experienced meant I had to learn to be kinder to myself. I had to realize that the people I love aren't evaluating me by asking, "What do I get out of this?" And even if they did, do you know what that answer would be?

Me.

And apparently, learning to believe that has required me to confront just how often I evaluate myself. If you ask any of the people closest to me, they will tell you I am my harshest critic. The me-versus-me becomes a *Celebrity Deathmatch* at times. I had a habit of turning life into tournaments.

Me versus who I used to be.

Me versus who I thought I should be.

Me versus some imaginary woman who was doing it better.

Me versus the version of myself who had more energy, more patience, more margin.

But if everything becomes a competition, someone always has to lose—including me. I compared myself to where I think I should be and to past versions of myself who seemed to operate "better," without accounting for the season I'm actually in.

Parenting made that especially obvious. Of course I could keep an HGTV-inspired environment before having two rambunctious boys. Overstimulation rarely happened when I was getting 8–10 hours of sleep! In parenting, I expected to become this impressive version of myself that was not sustainable. I created countless spreadsheets and checklists to detail not just what each kid needed but also what I thought they should have. I'd spend hours obsessing over cube storage and whether I should color-coordinate their drawers, when really, the best version of me would come after a nap.

Psalm 18:19 says: *"He brought me out into a spacious place; he rescued me because he delighted in me" (NIV).*

This verse reminds me that God isn't waiting on me to become impressive before He enjoys me.

Enough, then, becomes a gift rather than a goal. The garden doesn't ask me to prove I belong there tomorrow before I sit down today.

Session Summary

This chapter reminded us that participation isn't the absence of planning. It's the willingness to stop planning long enough to experience what the planning was supposed to make possible.

Reflection Questions

Question 1: Was there a moment when you realized, *"Wait...we're not behind. We're just not on my old schedule"*?

Question 2: What does enjoyment mean to you? Where in your life can you spend more time enjoying rather than evaluating?

Question 3: Where are you tempted to over-prepare, rush the timeline, or evaluate yourself—and what would it look like to participate instead?

Treatment Plan

Choose one area of your life where you notice yourself **preparing, predicting, or evaluating instead of participating**

Write down:

1. What am I hoping for?

Name the desire without attaching a deadline to it

2. What story am I telling myself about the timeline?

What am I assuming the timing means about me, God, or my future?

3. What is actually true right now?

Separate evidence from interpretation

4. What is here for me to participate in today?

Name one thing you can experience, enjoy, nurture, or receive **without needing it to become something else first**

Then finish with:

I can want ______ without needing it by ______.

Today, I am willing to participate in ______.

Chapter 5: Remaining

Stop Asking Today to Wear Tomorrow's Clothes

I hope this journey of becoming has taught us how to hold onto our hopes without demanding that today pretend to be tomorrow. That isn't passive waiting or settling. It's patience in action.

How often does anxiety walk into an ordinary Wednesday and say, "excuse me, why aren't you already Saturday?" Perhaps it makes us question why a six-month relationship doesn't feel like a three-year one. Why does the first year in a new job not feel like the tenth? Why does rebuilding a life not feel like an established one? Anxiety constantly asks today to wear tomorrow's clothes. No wonder today feels uncomfortable; those clothes don't fit yet!

Wise Mind would probably walk over, gently take tomorrow's jacket off today's shoulders, and say, "This is lovely, but today doesn't have to cosplay as the future!"

Imagine a 6-year-old putting on an adult's blazer. It's a good blazer. It's just not time yet. The sleeves hang past their hands. They trip over it. It swallows them up rather than letting them shine. It doesn't mean they'll never wear one. It simply means it's not their size yet. And so many of us experience this in our daily lives: we walk into today carrying tomorrow's wardrobe. We tell ourselves: "Wear the engagement ring now." "Wear the certainty now." "Wear the finished house now." Meanwhile, today is just trying to wear today's clothes.

No wonder we feel clumsy. We're trying to move around in garments that belong to another season. Hope doesn't ask today to wear tomorrow's clothes. Hope gets dressed for today and trusts tomorrow to arrive with a wardrobe of its own. Anxiety raids tomorrow's closet. Wisdom gets dressed for today.

There have been so many times in my life when my heart was asking today's chapter to show up as tomorrow. As a parent, I've cried out about how I can effectively show up for each child individually without losing myself. I've wanted to know the system, the schedule, the solution—the version of parenting where everyone is regulated, the house is functioning, and I still have something left at the end of the day. As a therapist, I've tried to harvest what my clients were still planting. I've had to stop, look in the mirror, and ask myself which day's clothes I was wearing. And it didn't invalidate the longing I had to care for others; it just gently asked me whether today was carrying a weight it was never meant to carry.

God so often gives enough for today. God gave the Israelites manna each day. Jesus taught us to pray for our daily bread. Not because tomorrow doesn't matter. Because today's grace is tailored to today's shoulders. Tomorrow's grace will fit tomorrow. Different wardrobe. Same faithful God. Today doesn't have to prove tomorrow. It only has to be faithful to today.

Matthew 6:34 reminds us: *"Therefore do not worry about tomorrow, for tomorrow will worry about itself. Each day has enough trouble of its own." (NIV)*

That's what I've been discovering. Not that today has to be tomorrow. But that today can faithfully prepare you for it. I stopped asking today's chapter to contain the whole book, and I stopped treating my life like a mystery novel I had to solve.

The Difference Between Acknowledging and Solving

I remember a conversation I had with a friend when I was processing a recent update. Someone I love dearly was supposed to move closer, but their move date was delayed. I started the conversation thinking, "I'm anxious because the timeline changed." We had plans and activities that seemed to fade into unknown calendars right before my eyes. But by the end of our conversation, I realized it wasn't just anxiety, but grief. I was sad because my heart hoped for something sooner. Two emotional tasks existed at the same time—anxiety was asking for certainty, while grief was asking for compassion.

And once I named my grief, my entire nervous system seemed to soften. Not because the circumstances automatically improved, but because I stopped trying to solve a loss that really just needed to be acknowledged. There was something so freeing in that because when we mistake grief for a problem, we immediately start looking for a solution. But grief isn't a math equation. It's a love equation. You only grieve what mattered. Those are completely different workloads. One requires omniscience. The other requires tissues.

Grief asks a very different question than anxiety. Anxiety asks: "How do I stop this from happening?" Grief asks: "Can someone sit with me while I acknowledge what I hoped for?" Think about the last time you experienced disappointment or loss. If you asked a friend to come over, were you asking for certainty or consolation?

And to all my fellow helpers around the world, this is where we can really fall into a subtle trap. We become so good at meaning-making that we accidentally skip mourning. We move straight to: What's the reframe? What's the growth? What is God teaching me? And while those are all valuable questions, they aren't always the best answer. Sometimes the first faith response is simply: "Lord, I really wanted that." Not because your faith is weak. But because your hope was real.

And this same pattern can show up in our relationships. Sometimes we don't just try to solve our own pain—we try to solve someone else's.

Can I step into the judgment-free zone real quick? *Hi, my name is Rachael, and I am a recovering control freak.* But I promise, it came from a good place. Control felt like fixing and solving, especially in past relationships when I observed inconsistency and mistook it for a lack of capacity. When someone was inconsistent, control felt protective. But when someone is already living according to who they are and what they have the capacity to give, control becomes unnecessary. I don't have to manage someone into becoming someone they're not. I can pay attention to who they are and decide how I want to respond.

And friend, I get it. Sitting with someone and not solving the problem can be so frustrating! But who told us that sitting with someone was doing nothing? Perhaps it's that outdated software that taught our nervous systems to confuse action with love. For me, the urge to rescue was love trying to outrun helplessness. But love doesn't always outrun helplessness. Sometimes love sits in the passenger seat while someone you trust drives through their own hard season.

I've literally made a career out of sitting with people in crisis and helping them find their footing. Of course my nervous system would conclude, "If someone I love hurts, I should do something." But there are some hurts that don't need fixing. Helplessness is one of the prices of intimacy. You cannot love someone deeply and never have to watch them struggle. I don't think God is teaching us to become less loving. I think He's teaching us the difference between carrying someone and accompanying them. And you don't have to be a therapist to have a savior complex. Holy Spirit Jr. shows up in all of us from time to time. A savior says, "Here's what I'm going to do." A healthy partner, friend, or parent can ask, "How can I best show up?" Sometimes the most loving thing isn't offering the solution. It's allowing someone the dignity of finding their own way through it.

And that realization forced me to confront a harder question: If I can't control the outcome, then what am I actually responsible for? Not the timeline. Not another person's choices. Not whether everything turns out the way I hoped. I am responsible for how I remain connected to God in the middle of it. And that's where I began to understand fruit differently. Fruit isn't proof that I managed everything correctly. It's evidence of connection. A branch doesn't strain to manufacture fruit. It remains connected to the Vine, and fruit grows from that connection.

Fruit Is Evidence of Connection, Not Control

I realized my job is not to make the fruit happen, but to remain connected. Fruit becomes the outcome, not the assignment. I've learned to trust that remaining can be more sustaining than striving, and connection can be more sustaining than vigilance. So perhaps the greatest act of faith isn't always working harder. Sometimes it's relaxing back into the Vine.

You don't have to manufacture fruit to prove the connection is real. In fact, trying to force the fruit can become another form of control. The fruit isn't evidence that I successfully controlled the outcome. It's evidence of what happens when I remain connected to the Vine.

Jesus says in John 15 that the branch cannot bear fruit by itself; it must remain connected to the vine. I used to only read that as a spiritual instruction. Now I hear it differently. It is also an invitation to stop treating fruit as something I have to manufacture.

In my faith journey it has been very easy to confuse spiritual activity with spiritual connection. The often-churchy answer to "how is your faith walk going?" usually centered on which devotional I was reading, which small group I attended, which ministry I served in, or which service I attended. But connection was really found in the moments I sat with God when I didn't know the answers; tears streaming down my cheeks as I washed dishes, silent screams in the shower when I got my first free moment of the day, or even regulating breaths so that I could respond calmly to a kid calling my name 10 times. Connection met me when I was beyond capacity for action.

As you have learned about me in these pages, I am the quintessential Bob the Builder™, Bobbina, if you will, for my own life. His theme song "Can we fix it?!" became a personal challenge for me. I carry so many expectations of what I should have "fixed" by now, when once again I am only being asked to be connected. It doesn't mean I'm not capable. It means even the best power tool has to remain connected to a source to be most effective.

Fruit isn't the same thing as getting the outcome I wanted. A relationship ending doesn't mean there was no fruit. A season of waiting doesn't mean nothing grew. A project changing direction doesn't mean the work was wasted. Sometimes the fruit is patience. Sometimes it's wisdom. Sometimes it's courage. Sometimes it's the capacity to love differently than you did before. Sometimes the fruit is simply who you became while you were waiting.

As we temporarily leave our garden together, I want to leave you with a few of my favorite plaques I've created throughout my own garden:

Stay Connected and You'll Be Sustained

I Am Not Responsible for Securing the Garden, Just Relaxing in It

Participation Is Not the Same Thing as Preparation

Fruit Is Evidence of Connection, Not Control

The Next Chapter Does Not Require Me to Drag It Into Existence

My Confidence Is Not in the Absence of Storms. It's in the Presence of the Gardener

If I Never Relax, I Might Be Blinded to Joy

The garden was never asking me to control the harvest. It was inviting me to remain. And so my final question to you is: "You coming?"

Session Summary

This chapter wasn't about learning how to stop hoping, planning, grieving, or caring. It was about learning to participate in the life that exists while allowing the life you hope for to unfold in its own time.

Reflection Questions

Question 1: Where in your life are you currently asking for certainty about the future instead of allowing yourself to be present with what is true today?

Question 2: When was the last time you paused to acknowledge a hard loss or season? Spend some time sitting with that version of yourself, and consider what it means to offer compassion instead of certainty.

Question 3: What does being fruitful mean to you? What are you connected to that allows you to grow?

Treatment Plan

Take some time to think about the various areas of your life—family, friendships, relationships, work, faith, or personal growth. Create a "Garden Plaque" for each area that reminds you how you want to remain connected rather than control the outcome.

Bonus: Find a creative way to make these tangible objects. You can print them, draw them with markers, create them digitally, or make a photo collage using magazines and/or family photos. Place them somewhere you'll actually see them.

Alright, my friend, exhale.

The garden doesn't need you to manage every inch of it.

Go enjoy it.

Participate.

Acknowledgments

There are so many people who truly made this vision a reality. First, to God, my Lord, Savior, and the most loving Gardener I know—thank You for this opportunity. May You get all the glory and may our lives and minds be changed by Your love.

To my amazing publishing coach Nina Addison—thank you from the bottom of my heart for your prayers, words of encouragement, and believing in my crazy timelines. Thank you for not letting me quit or delay when life handed me a doozy. May God bless the works of your hands one hundredfold.

Thank you to my Dad, my stepmom Audry, and my brother Greg who kept the boys busy at the park or at home so I could squeeze in writing time. Your support in this season has truly been life-changing and I am so blessed to have you in my life. Thank you for being a faithful presence.

Thank you to Mama Cynn and Papa Norm for your continued prayers, excitement, and willingness to change your travel plans to support me. I know I'm your favorite child and now it's in writing ;)

Thank you to my children Mya, Caleb, and Joshua who inspire me daily to be present. Your joy, humor, and genuine delight in life give me purpose.

Thank you to my friends who have encouraged me, prayed for me, helped me pick cover designs, author pictures, and so much more. Jamarr, Lesley, Allie, Keyz, and GiGi—thank you for being safe spaces in some of my toughest seasons—I love you and appreciate you beyond words.

*The sunflower illustrations throughout this book were created with the assistance of OpenAI's ChatGPT and are original AI-generated artwork created for this publication.

www.ingramcontent.com/pod-product-compliance
Lightning Source LLC
LaVergne TN
LVHW021736071126
851857LV00040B/1469
* 9 7 9 8 2 3 4 1 6 3 2 4 0 *